PROTECT YOUR DATA AND IDENTITY ONLINE

by A. R. Carser

BrightP◆int Press

San Diego, CA

BrightPoint Press

© 2022 BrightPoint Press
an imprint of ReferencePoint Press, Inc.
Printed in the United States

For more information, contact:
BrightPoint Press
PO Box 27779
San Diego, CA 92198
www.BrightPointPress.com

LIBRARY OF CONGRESS CATALOGING-IN-PUBLICATION DATA

Names: Carser, A. R., author.
Title: Protect Your Data and Identity Online / by A. R. Carser.
Description: San Diego, CA : BrightPoint Press, [2022] | Series: Protect yourself online |
　Includes bibliographical references and index. | Audience: Grades 7-9
Identifiers: ISBN 9781678202507 (hardcover) | ISBN 9781678202514 (eBook)
The complete Library of Congress record is available at www.loc.gov.

CONTENTS

AT A GLANCE   4

INTRODUCTION   6
AN UNEXPECTED WHISPER

CHAPTER ONE   14
WHO HAS YOUR DATA?

CHAPTER TWO   30
THE HISTORY OF PROTECTING
PERSONAL DATA

CHAPTER THREE   46
WARNING SIGNS

CHAPTER FOUR   60
HOW TO PROTECT PERSONAL DATA

Glossary   74
Source Notes   75
For Further Research   76
Index   78
Image Credits   79
About the Author   80

AT A GLANCE

- Personal data is information that can be used to identify a person. This includes details like a person's full name, birth date, and address. It can also include a Social Security number or bank account information.

- Cybercriminals can steal a person's identity by stealing his or her personal data. They may resell this information to others. Or they may use it to open accounts, such as credit cards, in the victim's name.

- People can easily share personal data online. This can be done using social media, games, and websites that require an account.

- Companies with websites, games, and apps collect users' personal data. They want to learn more about the users. Companies may use this information to improve their products and services. They may also sell the information to other companies.

- Hundreds of millions of people have had their personal data stolen. This includes people under 18 years old.

- There are laws to protect young people's personal data. These laws protect against data being collected and used.

- If kids' personal data has been stolen, they may not want to tell an adult about their online activity. They may be afraid of getting into trouble. They might be ashamed. But adults will be able to help them.

AN UNEXPECTED WHISPER

"Finally!" Lucas thought as he emailed his essay to his teacher. He grabbed a drink. Then, he sat back down at his computer. His squad was waiting for him. He hopped on Discord. Discord was their voice and chat app. Lucas waited for *Fortnite* to load. He said hello to his buddies on Discord. Then, he

In-game chats can be fun. But sometimes strangers ask players for their private data.

checked his phone for messages on Party

Hub. Party Hub was *Fortnite*'s chat app.

Nothing new there. All he saw was trash

talk from another squad.

It's a smart idea for people to think twice before sharing personal information online.

Lucas and his friends won their first Battle Royale. Then, they took a five-minute break. Lucas checked the game chat. He had a message from a player he did not know. It read, "Dude, that was close at the end! You guys been playing together long? I bet you know each other IRL. Where are you from? I'm in Indiana."

Lucas was in Indiana too. However, he thought twice about sharing his location. He and his buddies had always played together. But why did this guy care about that? Then, he remembered what happened to his older brother. His brother shared his account information with someone in a game. That person stole Lucas's brother's identity. The issue took months to sort out, and his brother was unable to buy his first car.

Lucas shrugged. "It's probably nothing," he thought to himself. "But he doesn't need to know everything about us." He responded to the message by typing: "You bet, man! You guys played well too. You almost had us at the end." He left it at that.

BEING SMART ABOUT PERSONAL DATA

Lucas was smart not to share information. Chat is a helpful tool for gamers.

Smartphones are a great way to connect with others. But people need to be careful not to share personal data online.

But sometimes people use chat apps

and social media for bad reasons. They

try to learn personal information about

others. Personal information is details

about someone's identity. It can include

his or her full name and location. Birthdays and **Social Security numbers** are also personal data. Some people use personal data to harm others. They may sell the information to criminals.

Gaming and social media companies collect personal data. So do other companies. They use these details to learn more about how people use their products and services. They may also sell data to other companies.

Being online with friends helps people stay connected. People can make sure they

Using secure passwords is one way people can protect their personal data.

stay safe too. Protecting personal data is

not difficult. But it is a serious responsibility.

CHAPTER ONE

WHO HAS YOUR DATA?

People share personal data online all the time. They cannot completely avoid sharing it. But they can be smart. They can decide what personal details they share. They can choose who they share it with. People can decide when to share data.

Many social media apps tag a person's location when she shares a post. These app settings can be changed so personal data is kept private.

BEWARE WHAT'S SHARED

Sometimes, people share personal data on purpose. They share their address with a store. It helps them make a purchase. They use their email address to create an online account. Other times, people share data accidentally. This could happen when they share a photo. Information could be visible in the photo. Or a social media app may tag their location. They may tell strangers in a game it is their birthday.

Sharing personal data online takes just a second or two. Once shared, that data is online forever. This is true even when people

Identity thieves use personal data to access bank accounts. This allows them to withdraw money or make purchases on the victim's account.

delete posts or photos. It is even true if they

delete accounts. Companies may keep

records of past user data. It is also possible

for other users to save information. They

may keep screenshots of photos. They

could write down birthdays.

Some people share a lot of information

online. This makes it easier to steal it.

People may use stolen data to harm others.

For example, bullies may save pictures or

WHAT YOUNG PEOPLE WANT TO KNOW

Most young people know using the internet is
risky. A survey asked 165 children in the United
Kingdom about personal data. Most wanted to
know when and how a company collects their
data. They wanted to opt out of data collection.
Many wanted to know where their deleted data
goes. They also wanted companies to act faster
to remove harmful content.

videos. They may use these to cause social or emotional harm. Criminals could steal personal data. They might use that data to access bank accounts. They may use it to open new accounts. This is called identity theft. It causes financial harm. It affects more than a million Americans every year. This includes adults and children.

WHO COLLECTS PERSONAL DATA ONLINE?

Criminals and bullies look for personal data on social media. They may ask another user to share personal details. They may ask for a person's full name in game chat.

Or they may ask someone to share his or her location in an email. A criminal may ask someone to download a program. The program allows the criminal to gain access to the user's computer. "Direct messages are popular places for cyber thieves who place links to . . . harmful downloads for kids," according to Luis Corron. Corron works for the National Cyber Security Alliance.[1] Some criminals pose as children. This makes other users feel safe. Then it is easier for criminals to obtain personal information.

Thieves hack victims' computers to obtain their personal information.

Websites collect data from their customers.

Other criminals steal personal data.

Thieves may hack an online game. They

may trick a gamer into entering a username

and password. From there, they can access

the gamer's account. Then they can steal

the gamer's personal data.

Some people collect data legally.

Companies collect data on website

users. They use this data to improve their

websites. Retailers may keep someone's

purchase history. They use it to recommend

new products. Social media companies use

personal information to sell ads. A school

laptop may collect student data. The laptop

uses the data to track student learning.

Data **brokers** collect personal data.

The brokers sell it to other companies.

Thorin Klosowski is a *New York Times*

THE DARK WEB

When most people use the internet, they visit lawful websites. They behave as good internet citizens. But criminals use an illegal network. It is called the dark web. There, they buy and sell stolen personal data. They also buy and sell other illegal items. Stolen personal data often ends up for sale on the dark web. Criminals buy the data to create accounts. They make purchases with stolen bank details. A young person's data is especially attractive. Most young people have clean financial histories. It is easy to use their personal data illegally.

columnist. He explains, "Data brokers collect information from everywhere they can, including public records, commercial sources, and Web browsing."[2] Brokers compile a user's data. They make educated guesses about the user based on this data. They guess about the user's likes and dislikes. They guess about religious and political values. They sell this information to other companies. The other companies use it for advertising.

DATA FROM DEVICES

Most people expect the websites they visit to collect data. But devices collect data too.

Smart home technologies collect data every time someone uses them. This includes Amazon's Alexa and Google Home. Adam Wright is a senior analyst. He works at the marketing technology firm IDC. He explained the issue to *Vox*. He said, "Most smart home devices give . . . vendors a view into the device's location, performance, operating state, and the frequency which a user is interacting with it, and in what ways."[3] All this information is a form of personal data.

Other kinds of devices gather data too. Video streaming devices gather viewing

Smart home devices can make life easier for people. But they collect their owners' personal data too.

Fitness devices help people measure their health and fitness goals. They also track users' data.

data from users. Smart watches such

as the Apple Watch collect health data.

Personal fitness devices such as Fitbits

do too. Game consoles and toys that

use wireless internet connections collect

data. Data brokers may gather this data.

They use it to create a profile for a user or

a family.

CHAPTER TWO

THE HISTORY OF PROTECTING PERSONAL DATA

Protecting personal data online has been a widespread concern since 1993. That is when the **World Wide Web** became public. Since then, people have tried to keep personal data safe. Companies, schools, and government

Data breaches can cost companies millions of dollars.

agencies work to protect data. They try to

prevent data theft.

A COMMON PROBLEM

Personal data theft is common. The largest **data breach** ever involved 3 billion people. That was the breach of Yahoo. Yahoo is a web service and email provider. The breach happened in 2013. Since then, hundreds of millions of people have had their data stolen. In 2020, the average total cost of a single data breach to a company was $3.86 million.

Most stolen data is the personal information of adults. However, young people also have their data stolen. Approximately 1.3 million children have their identities stolen every year. Most victims are

under six years old. Children do not work.

They do not make credit card purchases.

WHAT'S A CREDIT REPORT?

A credit report is a record of a person's credit history. It shows the number of loans the person has taken out. It proves the person has repaid those loans or paid bills on time. A credit report rates each person with a number called a credit score. Companies use credit reports when deciding whether to lend money to people. People with poor credit may not get a loan for a home. They may not be able to rent an apartment. They may not be able to borrow money to purchase a car. Some companies use credit scores to decide who to hire. It is important to check credit reports regularly. People can see if someone else is taking out loans in their name.

Criminals use victims' Social Security numbers to steal their identities.

Their credit histories are blank. Few parents check their children's credit histories. Criminals can use a child's identity for years before being discovered. By that time, a child's credit history could be ruined. This could make it difficult to buy a car in the future. It could hurt the person's chances of getting a student loan.

The federal government tries to protect the personal data of young people. One law protects the data of young people in foster care. It is called the Foster Youth Financial Security Act of 2011. It requires states to stop using a child's Social Security number.

This reduces the number of times the Social Security number gets shared. States had used these numbers to identify children in their systems. The law also requires states to give people in foster care their credit reports. State workers must help them repair stolen credit histories.

Another law protects young people under the age of thirteen. It is called the Children's Online Privacy Protection Act (COPPA). COPPA limits how companies can use the data of their younger users. It was enacted in 1998. It applies to companies who run websites and apps for children under age thirteen. It also applies to toy

and game companies. Companies offering

services to both kids and adults must

comply with COPPA. Companies must

share their privacy policies with users. They

must tell parents how they use children's

A REAL-LIFE COPPA EXAMPLE

Many young people run into COPPA online.
They might not even realize it. Some websites
ask users to confirm they are over thirteen
years old. This is COPPA in action. Many
sites require account holders to be over
this age. These websites include Facebook,
Instagram, and YouTube. Limiting users by age
helps them avoid blame for improperly using
children's data.

personal data. Companies must have a
system to protect the personal data of
young people. They must delete data after
they no longer need it.

PERSONAL DATA BREACHES IN THE NEWS

In 2017, experts discovered something on
the dark web. The personal information for
hundreds of thousands of children was for
sale. Half a million records had been stolen
from pediatricians' offices. Approximately
200,000 had been stolen from schools. The
data sold for an average of $3.00 on the
dark web.

Millions of people have had their credit card data stolen in data breaches.

That same year, Equifax became the victim of a data breach. Equifax is a **credit bureau**. It stores the personal and financial data of millions of adults. Approximately 147.9 million people had their personal data

Cybercriminals stole personal data from users of the online game Words with Friends.

stolen. The data included Social Security numbers and birth dates. It also included addresses and credit card data.

In 2018, criminals stole data from the app MyFitnessPal. Approximately 150 million users were affected. The same year, video messaging service Dubsmash was attacked. Thieves stole data from 162 million accounts. Personal data stolen from these breaches was sold on the dark web.

The next year, thieves attacked popular online game developer Zynga. Zynga created many popular mobile games.

Farmville and *Words with Friends* are among their games. Criminals stole email addresses, phone numbers, and passwords. The breach affected 218 million users.

PERSONAL DATA THEFT IN MEDIA

Many movies and TV shows feature online crimes. They show the dangers of sharing personal data. *Cyber Crime* was a 2019 documentary about personal data theft. *The Social Dilemma* came out in 2020. It discussed the effects social media has on users. In 2021, the documentary *Silk Road* premiered. It discussed the dark web

Many movies and TV shows have been made about cybercrimes.

DATA BREACHES IN THE NEWS

	Company Description	Date of Breach	Users Affected
Marriott International	Hotel	2014–2018	500 million
Zynga	Facebook gaming app	September 2019	218 million
Dubsmash	Video messenger	December 2018	162 million
MyFitnessPal	Fitness app	February 2018	150 million
Equifax	Credit bureau	July 2017	147.9 million
Canva	Graphic design app	May 2019	137 million

Source: Michael Hill and Dan Swinhoe, "The 15 Biggest Data Breaches of the 21st Century," CSO, July 16, 2021. www.csoonline.com.

Hundreds of millions of people are victims of data breaches every year. Many large data breaches make the news.

market Silk Road. The FBI shut down Silk

Road in 2013. Ross William Ulbricht had

operated Silk Road. He was sentenced to

life in prison for his crimes. Judge Katherine Forrest said, "You cannot run a massive criminal enterprise and, because it occurred over the internet, minimize the crime."[4]

The number of movies made about online dangers reflects how common data theft has become in real life. Protecting personal data is a challenge for internet users. Companies are getting better at preventing data theft. But criminals are getting better too. Users must learn to identify when their personal data may be stolen. They need to take steps to protect it.

CHAPTER THREE

WARNING SIGNS

P rotecting personal data online takes attention. People must think twice before they share information. They should avoid sharing personal data on social media. They should not share personal details in a game or on a website. Knowing the warning signs for data theft can help people stay safe.

Users cannot always control who sees their photos and videos online.

DATA RED FLAGS

Social media, online games, and chats are

public spaces. What people share on social

media lives online forever. The same is

true of in-game chat and direct messages. Users cannot completely control who can see their posts. They do not always decide who sees photos and videos. This makes sharing personal data online risky.

Many social media apps automatically make user profiles public. Anyone can

WAYS TO SPOT A SCAM

Spotting a personal data scam can be easy. Strangers may ask someone for a photo or video. A stranger may ask someone for his or her account details in a chat or email. Pop-ups may appear in a game or on a website. They could ask for an email address. Spotting and preventing data theft comes down to trust. Only share information with people you know and trust.

see the details users share. Users who

create live videos can unintentionally share

personal data. They may accidentally share

their names. Or they may share the names

of family and friends. Their backgrounds

may give away their locations. People may

share personal data in comments on posts

or private messages. Bullies and criminals

may see this data. They may encourage

users to share personal details with them.

They may use this data against users later.

It is possible for gamers to accidentally

share personal data too. Many games

have in-game chat. Players can talk with

each other. For other games, players use separate chat apps. Discord is one popular chat app. It can be easy to share personal data through game chat. A player might accidentally use her real name rather than her character's name. Or other players may press someone to share his location. They may ask how old he is. All of these things are red flags.

Many companies ask people for personal data. In exchange, these people can use the companies' websites. Users agree to a website's **cookies** policy before using the site. The same is true of privacy policies.

It can be easy for gamers to accidentally share personal data.

It is true of terms and conditions too.

Cookies track what users do on company

pages. This helps companies learn how

people use the website. It can also save

user data in a convenient way. Most

websites that collect user data have

privacy statements. These tell users what

ARM YOUR CHARACTER, ARM YOURSELF

Gaming is a fun way to spend time with people. Many games allow players to speak with strangers. An online world is a lot like the real world. Imagine if a stranger walked up to you in the park and asked for your name and address. You probably would not give out those details. The same should be true of a stranger in a game.

the websites do with their data. Terms and conditions policies also include these details. However, these are legal documents. They can be difficult to read. Many users agree to these policies without reading or understanding them.

Checking a credit report may reveal red flags. Young people should have clean credit histories. A credit report that shows unexpected credit card use and loans is worrisome. This could be a sign that a young person's identity has been stolen. Getting notices in the mail for overdue bills is another sign. Adults should take steps

Receiving overdue bills for unfamiliar purchases can be a sign that a person's identity has been stolen.

to fix these issues. "Don't assume it's a mistake," said Eva Velazquez. She is the president of the nonprofit Identity Theft

Resource Center. "You need to follow up on them right away," she added.[5]

EMERGING THREATS

New threats to personal data constantly appear. Many people use apps to tell personal stories. They think they are keeping their identities secret. Snapchat and Whisper are examples of these apps. But sharing private details often reveals personal data. This includes stories about emotional or social struggles. "Anonymous sharing can promote health and open expression for users. It can also make it easier to overshare information," according to Luis Corron.[6]

In 2020 and 2021, the COVID-19 pandemic occurred. It caused an increase in personal data and identity theft. These thefts affected young people. In March 2020, most schools changed from classroom learning to remote learning. Millions of students took classes online using learning apps. They used video software such as Zoom. In-person activities were canceled. Personal internet use increased. Cybercrimes against children rose. In the state of Tennessee, police

Internet use increased during the COVID-19 pandemic. As a result, cybercrimes increased too.

asked for tips on cybercrimes against kids.

They received more than twice the usual

number of tips.

Teens who fall victim to personal data theft should ask a trusted adult for help.

SPOTTING WHEN SOMEONE IS IN TROUBLE

Victims of personal data theft may show

warning signs. They may be afraid to share

what they have been doing on social media.

This may be because they are ashamed of being bullied. Or they may be afraid of getting into trouble. People might look nervous when they check social media. They could get anxious about a direct message or email. They may try to hide what they are doing online. Sometimes, they get defensive when asked about their online activity. They may seem angry or depressed.

In cases like these, it is a good idea to ask an adult for help. Preventing data theft is much easier than dealing with its consequences.

CHAPTER FOUR

HOW TO PROTECT PERSONAL DATA

It is important to understand why sharing personal data on the internet is risky. It is equally important to put that knowledge into action. It's easy to fall victim to personal data theft, but people can take steps to avoid this. They can do something when they believe their data has been stolen.

Social media users should be careful not to share personal details online.

Being careful online can reduce the

potential risks and harms of stolen data.

KEEP PERSONAL DATA SAFE

The first thing people can do is build good

online habits. Social media users should

think twice before posting a photo of their

birthday party. They should reconsider tagging their location. They should rethink sharing their friend's name. The same goes for making comments on someone else's posts. It is best not to share details in a direct message either. Pause to think about who will see the shared information. This can keep data safe.

It can be tempting to share login information with friends. But sharing usernames, passwords, and other account details is risky. Once someone shares this data, he or she no longer controls it. A friend may accidentally share the information with someone else. That

person may share it with another person.

Even riskier is sharing account details and

locations with strangers. A good habit is not

to share account details, full names, birth

dates, or locations with strangers. This is

especially true for strangers online.

CREATING SECURE USERNAMES

It can be easy to accidentally give away personal data in a username. Avoid using an email address or first or full name. The same goes for age, birth date, or other personal details. Instead, choose something without personal data. Make it inoffensive and clean too. This ensures the username will not offend someone. It also will not embarrass you later on.

Users should report stolen data, harassment, and bullying that they encounter online.

There is another thing people can do to protect their personal data. They can read websites' privacy policies. They can study a service's terms and conditions. These documents contain information on what companies do with user information. They also contain instructions on how users can report stolen information, bullying, and harassment. Reporting an issue is the first step to fixing it.

PREVENTING DATA THEFT

Preventing personal data theft is easier than recovering stolen data. People can limit the personal data they share. To do this, they can keep a list of the accounts they open online. This includes websites, social media, games, and apps. People should check their lists regularly. They can delete the accounts and apps they no longer use. But doing this doesn't mean your data has been deleted. People need to contact the online company to request to have this done. People should also consider whether they need to create a new account. They should think twice about downloading a new app.

Sometimes, it is necessary to open a new account. If so, a user should create a unique username and password

Using two-step verification adds an extra layer of security to online accounts and services.

for it. Another thing people can do is

use **two-step verification**. This is a

technology that requires two steps to log

into an account. First, the user enters the username and password. Then, the website or app sends the person a code. The code is sent as an email or text. The user needs to enter this code to access the account. Adding this step to the process makes it very difficult for thieves to steal data.

Users can also update their accounts' privacy settings. These settings help users restrict who sees their posts and photos. They decide who can contact them through an app. Other settings limit what data the account can gather. Some apps ask for details from a device. They ask for its location, contacts, and photos. They may request access to videos, calendars, and other data. Choosing not to share these things protects the user's personal data. It also protects the data of the people in the user's contact lists.

CREATING SECURE PASSWORDS

A strong password ensures an online account stays safe. Creating a secure password is easy. Start with a word or phrase. It should be at least eight characters long. Longer passwords are more difficult to guess. Nonsense words can make great passwords. An example may be a pet's nickname. Add a few numbers and symbols to your password. However, do not use your birthday, address, or phone number. These things are easier for thieves to guess.

A strong password keeps online accounts secure.

WHAT TO DO IF PERSONAL DATA IS STOLEN

Most social media sites and game apps

allow users to report problems. These

can include harassment or offensive

content. People can also report online bullies. Sometimes, accounts get hacked. If this happens, users need to take action. They should change their passwords. The hacked password could have been used on other accounts. Those accounts need unique passwords too. A password manager app can keep track of passwords. It creates very secure passwords. It is important to set a unique and secure password for a password manager account.

People who have lost personal data can get help. An adult can help them reset passwords. They can help set privacy settings. This makes sure personal data is not shared or stolen again. An adult can get someone's credit report. This will show if the person's identity has been stolen. "Generally, a child under 18 won't have a credit report unless someone is using his or her information for fraud," according to the Federal Trade Commission.[7]

Protecting personal data online is a serious responsibility. People may not realize personal details stay public online for years. This can be true even if they no longer use those accounts. Sharing personal data with strangers can put users

When people protect their private details online, they can safely use and enjoy apps, games, and websites.

in danger. This is why it is important to

protect personal data online. People can

understand the risks and be smart about

the information they share. They can protect

their data and identity online.

GLOSSARY

brokers

people who arrange the sale of something, such as personal data

cookies

small files that contain personal information about an internet user's online history

credit bureau

a business that collects individuals' financial information for banks and lenders to use

data breach

a leak of information from a company's data files, often caused by a cyberattack

Social Security numbers

a unique number each US citizen receives that is used for official federal government business

two-step verification

a method of online security that requires two different ways to confirm identity

World Wide Web

the system of connected pages that people can access using the internet

CHAPTER ONE: WHO HAS YOUR DATA?

1. Quoted in Luis Corron, "Social Cyber Threats Facing Children and Teens in 2018," *National Cyber Security Alliance*, January 17, 2018. www.staysafeonline.org.

2. Quoted in Thorin Klosowski, "Big Companies Harvest Our Data," *New York Times*, May 28, 2020. www.nytimes.com.

3. Quoted in Rani Molla, "People Say They Care About Privacy but They Continue to Buy Devices That Can Spy on Them," *Vox*, May 13, 2019. www.vox.com.

CHAPTER TWO: THE HISTORY OF PROTECTING PERSONAL DATA

4. Quoted in Benjamin Weiser, "Ross Ulbricht, Creator of Silk Road Website, Is Sentenced to Life in Prison," *New York Times*, May 29, 2015. www.nytimes.com.

CHAPTER THREE: WARNING SIGNS

5. Quoted in Herb Weisbaum, "More than 1 Million Children Were Victims of ID Theft," *NBC News*, June 21, 2018. www.nbcnews.com.

6. Quoted in Luis Corron, "Social Cyber Threats Facing Children and Teens in 2018," *National Cyber Security Alliance*, January 17, 2018. www.staysafeonline.org.

CHAPTER FOUR: HOW TO PROTECT PERSONAL DATA

7. Quoted in "How to Protect Your Child from Identity Theft," *Federal Trade Commission Consumer Information*, April 2021. www.consumer.ftc.gov.

FOR FURTHER RESEARCH

BOOKS

Carrie Anton, *A Smart Girl's Guide: Digital World: How to Connect, Share, Play, and Keep Yourself Safe*. Middleton, WI: American Girl, 2017.

Goali Saedi Bocci, *The Social Media Workbook for Teens: Skills to Help You Balance Screen Time, Manage Stress, and Take Charge of Your Life*. Oakland, CA: Instant Help Books, 2019.

J. K. O'Sullivan, *Online Scams*. San Diego, CA: BrightPoint Press, 2022.

INTERNET SOURCES

"Identity Theft Isn't Just an Adult Problem. Kids Are Victims, Too," *CNBC*, 2018. www.cnbc.com.

"Protecting Your Online Identity and Reputation," *TeensHealth*, 2018. www.kidshealth.org.

"Video Game Security: How to Stay Safer While Gaming," *Norton*, 2021. www.norton.com.

WEBSITES

Common Sense Media
www.commonsensemedia.org

This site is written for parents, but it has very useful information for young people too. Visit the site to discover how to set strong passwords and change account privacy settings.

Internet Matters for Teens
www.internetmatters.org/advice/14plus

Get an internet safety checklist to see if your online habits make the grade.

National Cyber Security Alliance
https://staysafeonline.org/stay-safe-online/managing-your -privacy/privacy-tips-teens

This nonprofit organization provides tips for teens to help them protect their privacy online.

INDEX

advertising, 25
apps, 4, 6–7, 11, 16, 36, 41, 44, 48, 50, 55–56, 66, 68, 70–71

breaches, 32, 38–39, 41–42, 44
brokers, 24–25, 29

Children's Online Privacy Protection Act (COPPA), 36–37
cookies, 50, 52
COVID-19 pandemic, 56
credit reports, 33, 36, 53, 72
cybercrimes, 56–57

dark web, 24, 38, 41–42
data theft, 31–32, 42, 45–46, 48, 58–60, 65
devices, 25–26, 29, 68
direct messages, 20, 48, 59, 62
Discord, 6, 50
downloads, 20

email addresses, 16, 42, 48, 63

Fortnite, 6–7
fraud, 72

hacking, 71

identity theft, 19, 54, 56
Instagram, 37, 47

password manager, 71
passwords, 23, 42, 62, 66, 68–69, 71
personal information, 11, 20, 23, 32, 38
privacy settings, 68
privacy statements, 52

screenshots, 18
smart home technologies, 26
Snapchat, 55
social media, 4, 11–12, 16, 19, 23, 42, 46–48, 58–59, 61, 66, 70
Social Security numbers, 4, 12, 35–36, 41

tag, 16, 62
technology, 26, 67
two-step verification, 67

usernames, 23, 62–63, 66, 68

Zoom, 56

IMAGE CREDITS

ABOUT THE AUTHOR

A. R. Carser is a freelance writer who lives in Minnesota. She enjoys learning and writing about cybercrime and internet safety.